Have Bags, Will Travel

Trips and Tales - Memoirs of an Over-packer

Trade paperback release: September 2015
ISBN: 978-0-9920974-9-3

Digitally published: September 2015
ISBN: Mobi 978-0-9947938-0-5
ISBN: Epub 978-0-9947938-1-2

Disclaimer

Have Bags, Will Travel is a work of nonfiction. It was written
using the author's opinions and recollections of events that took
place in her life, conveyed from her point of view. The author has
changed and omitted some names in her stories to maintain the
anonymity of some people mentioned.

Dedication

I dedicate this book to my besties, Bri
and Zan, for rolling with me through the
decades in good times and bad.

Acknowledgments

I'd like to once again thank my friend and author/ editor Deborah A. Bowman for her time and witty feedback during the final stages of putting this book together. And I'd also like to thank author and friend Deborah Jay for reading and for sharing her time and feedback on this book while in its earlier stages.

Editor: Talia Leduc
Cover Design: Yvonne Less, diversepixel.com
Book Design: jdsmith-design.com
Ebook Formatting: Biddlesebooks

Also Written by D.G. Kaye

Words We Carry
Essays of Obsession and Self-Esteem

MenoWhat? A Memoir
Memorable Moments of Menopause

Conflicted Hearts
A Daughter's Quest for Solace from Emotional Guilt

Editorial Review

"An honest MUST-READ memoir (psst…it WILL fit in your carry-on tote or purse!) filled with solid advice for the uninitiated and nostalgia for the seasoned traveler. An endearing whirlwind jaunt with the humor, wit, and good ol' common sense we've come to expect from the fiery-haired shopaholic author, D.G. Kaye!"

—Deborah A. Bowman, advanced clinical psychological hypnotherapist (ACPH), author of the Denny Ryder Paranormal Crime Series

"Travel, shopping, fabulous locations—and an insider tip on where to buy the best-priced designer shoes. What more could a girl want?"

—Deborah Jay, author of the epic fantasy *The Prince's Man* and *Desprite Measures*, a Caledonian Sprite urban fantasy

Contents

Introduction

What's more exciting than going on vacation? We all look forward to and dream about, at one time or another, a great escape. Whether to sand, land, or sea, it's always nice to get away. I love to travel. In my younger days, I went as far as taking a course to become a certified travel agent just so I could get discounts and perks for my own personal use.

Looking back into the past, however, I have to admit that I became more of a certified shopaholic than anything. Aside from the thrill of traveling to new destinations, the possibility of finding exciting purchases to bring back home with me certainly added to my enjoyment of a journey.

The biggest task in preparing for those jaunts was trying to solve the mystery of how I was going to fit everything I needed into my weight-restricted luggage. Then, inevitably, there was always the dilemma of how I was going to transport all my newfound treasures home without exceeding the permitted legal limits of either the airlines or Canada customs.

In today's times, it's become a bit more difficult to dance around these guidelines, with newer enforced weight restrictions and liquid and gel allowances. Also, trying to blend into a crowd of passengers on my return trips so I can sail through customs without being singled out as a person of interest is becoming increasingly difficult. Are you one of those people who're repeatedly chosen to be interrogated by customs when you return home from your vacations? Surely, it can't just be me!

These little obstacles haven't deterred my passion for travel, though, and I've become a more savvy packer with each trip. London, Paris, Rome…and, of course, my beloved Las Vegas: I've been to many places. As I reminisce about some of those vacations, I realize that each had its own memorable moments and hiccups, especially when it came to baggage issues and getting my purchases home. I've had to come up with some crafty packing tactics to overcome some of those pitfalls to support my over-indulgences when it comes to shopping.

In this book, while strolling through my memories of some of my more notable vacations, you may find some of the things we were permitted to do on an aircraft in earlier decades bizarre, and be reminded of simpler times when traveling was a joy. You may even find some of the dilemmas I've encountered in most of my adventures to be helpful in your own packing, and you may want to use some of my handy (but possibly unethical) strategies for planning your next trip.

Packing in a Simpler Time

As a gal who has traveled a lot, I can honestly say that I used to enjoy the thrill of the journey as much as the destination itself. Nowadays, preparing for a vacation has become an anxiety-driven ritual. Back in the day, packing for a trip to Florida was a breeze. On the other hand, a trip to, say, Europe involved a little more savvy knowhow when it came to packing.

These days, a flight to anywhere involves some crafty calculations. Okay, so maybe I've downplayed my Florida packing a bit—because packing for anywhere seems to involve a lot of thought for me, no matter how near or far my destination, for one day or one month. I carefully plot out which shoes and purses will match which clothes. Do I have enough underwear? Should I pack extras?

My bathroom toiletries are essential and plentiful, and they'll most definitely be coming along with me on every journey. Oh, yes, I'm the girl you can come to on any given trip if you need anything from Band-Aids to rubbing alcohol, Gravol to antacids, and even a particular size of safety pin. I'll most likely have whatever it is you need. I'm always prepared.

I was a lot worse when I was younger. I used to take the biggest suitcase ever made, and it was always full. So what if I thought I might need to change my outfit three times a day? God forbid someone see me sporting the same clothes twice. I didn't want anyone talking bad about me.

Certainly my over-packing strategies from days past have had to be streamlined, somewhat, to accommodate today's regulations on luggage allowance. It's an ongoing challenge trying to decide what I want to take with me and what I must now leave behind. Suffice it to say, I strive to keep up to date on the ever-changing baggage restriction guidelines so that I am prepared ahead of time, not wanting to encounter any unpleasant surprises once I'm ready to check in at the airport.

The Airlines of Yesteryear

I can't recall taking one trip with my husband without blurting out in complaint, "Whatever happened to the days of Wardair?" Every time we're seated on an airplane, packed in like sardines in our little cramped space, it takes me back to the days of yore, and I lament for the lost thrill of travel. Do you remember when aisles were wide enough to accommodate people to walk through them with their belongings without having to hit seated passengers in the face?

It was a different time, not like today, before the airlines crammed in as many seats as they legally could, leaving the aisles with barely a spare inch for the flight attendants to push a cart through. Quite often, they even bop you on the head if you aren't sitting erect. I'm sure many people can attest to sitting in an aisle seat and dozing off only to be startled awake by a sudden body check by a passing cart or a passenger en route to the bathroom. I'm often uncomfortable in those seats—and I have short legs.

When I was a child, Wardair was one of the best. We used to fly with them when we went on our family vacations to Florida. The seats were wide and comfortable, food and drinks were free, washrooms could actually accommodate full-size humans, and, lest we forget, there were smoking sections. We packed what we needed and wanted, with no worries about too much luggage or accidentally packing any liquids or gels in our carry-ons.

When I speak about food, I mean real food, not the prepackaged reheated sandwiches and wilted salads you can purchase today. Wardair served delicious hot meals on china dishes.

While I'm on the topic of yesteryear, I have to ask, what the heck was anyone thinking to allow smoking on an aircraft flying 32,000 feet in the air with no fire escape? Talk about a health hazard! Let's just forget for one moment that all passengers were subjected to recirculating second-hand smoke from more than half the passengers. What was one to do if someone dropped his cigarette and set the surrounding seats ablaze?

I'm almost positive there must also be a huge decline in membership in the mile-high club these days. The club may even be defunct now, with the lack of space in airplane washrooms for just one person, not to mention the ongoing line-ups for the toilets, as there's usually only one in the front and one in the back. Incidentally, I never joined that club, but I can tell you that even though I'm not a big person, paying a visit to the washroom involves a contortionist act.

I try to avoid using airplane washrooms as long as I can hold it, but when I absolutely have to relieve myself, I resort to this ritual: I first inch in sideways to avoid getting my shirt wet from the splashed water all around the sink. Pulling my pants down and holding them off the wet floor with one hand while the other supports my squat has become an acquired talent.

Washing my hands and avoiding germs from taps and the door handle are another part of the mission. I lather up with soap and hit the taps, but they only remain on for about three seconds, so you have to be quick. If I don't get all the soap off in record time, I manipulate my elbow for another hit of water. I dry my hands with a paper towel (if available) or a ream of toilet paper, which I also use to open the door handle while pushing with my shoulder, again avoiding the wet sink. I then drop the used paper in the garbage chute on the way out.

Sheesh, it's exhausting! Is it any wonder I avoid going to the washroom as long as I can hold out? Hey, germs are germs, and I don't think they were any friendlier in earlier times, but at least there was more room to move around in airplane washrooms.

Admitted Germ Freak

My germophobic tendencies don't only apply to airplanes. I admit it, I'm a germ freak. I'm afraid of them, and I'll go to any lengths to protect myself from them. It's not difficult to maintain this practice at home, but I can tell you I become a lot craftier in my crusade against germs once I'm outside the house.

My kitchen is well equipped with paper towels, cutting boards, and tea tree oil. When I'm preparing chicken, I'll wash it and place it on a non-wooden cutting board, which always hangs slightly over the counter and sink so no drops of *E. coli* or *Salmonella* fall on my counter. I immediately wash my hands and scour the sink before going on to the next steps. And no, I don't touch the faucet handle with my chicken hands, either. That's what the backs of my hands are for. Until that chicken is in a pan, ready to cook, I will wash my hands several times.

When I'm out and about, it's the public doors and shopping cart handles I'm on guard about. I treat public washrooms the same way I do airplane washrooms, only I'm grateful there's much more room to move around in the former. Wintertime makes touching things a lot easier, as I'm usually wearing gloves, but I still do my best to avoid door handles. If someone else is near, heading in my direction, I'll let that person go first and open the door. If I'm alone, I'll most likely use my shirt or coat to grasp the handle.

In the case of germy shopping carts, I sometimes have to succumb to touching them if I don't have my handy wipes with me or if I'm not wearing gloves, but the ample supply of hand sanitizer in my purse allevi-ates those situations. I'll pour it on my hands before getting in my car and touching my steering wheel. This may sound obsessive, but I try to avoid getting sick at all costs.

I go through my usual rituals when I travel, espe-cially when I first get into my hotel room. In my arsenal of germ defenses, I have a container of disinfecting wipes, so as soon as I set my bags down, I begin my routine. Hotel rooms are notorious for germs—some the average person doesn't even consider. I first tackle all the door handles, including drawer knobs, taps, and the toilet flusher. I then proceed to wipe down all the lamp and light switches, the radio buttons, the tele-phone and its number pad, and especially the remote control for the TV. Do I really need to explain why? Let me sum it up in one sentence: thousands of people have stayed in those rooms, and many don't wash their hands after going to the bathroom. 'Nuff said.

I never use the drinking glasses in the room for fear they were merely rinsed or, worse yet, cleaned with the same cloth used to wipe the toilet seat. Yuck! Surely you've seen the odd investigative show on TV where they do random checks on the cleanliness of hotel rooms?

Even before the vacation starts, plentiful germs are sometimes hard to avoid on airplanes. Planes are contained quarters filled with people hacking and sneezing—and many of them haven't learned to cover their mouths. Those germs circulate and distribute themselves through the recycled air, and where they land is anyone's guess.

While flying, you'll notice me lifting my shirt to cover my mouth and nose. This can become quite tiresome on a long flight, however, so I sometimes succumb to the environment. After I return home, about a day or two after leaving myself at the mercy of fate, I get a cold or flu. I've contemplated wearing a mask, but for more than just reasons of vanity, I haven't yet. Somewhere in my over-imaginative brain, I always think that if I'm the only one wearing a mask, people will think I have some awful contagious disease.

I wouldn't classify myself as obsessive compulsive, but I do get grossed out easily, and my regime is mainly about avoiding getting sick. Even if it is considered a compulsion, I'm calling it a lifestyle as opposed to a disorder. Hey, whatever it takes to feel comfortable, I'll do it!

Airport Security

It's no secret that the joy I once found in traveling has pretty much been obliterated. Traveling for me has now become a disciplined course on efficient packing and requires a good memory and some adequate math skills. I'm constantly reminding myself to pack all my liquids and gels in my checked luggage, and the same pertains to sharp objects such as scissors (for quick trims or for cutting price tags off newly purchased items I may plan on forgetting to claim at customs).

I have to remember to put my liquids in bottles of less than 100 mL in a plastic bag if I'm carrying them with me to make sure they aren't confiscated. Now I just have to remember to take out my little plastic bag from my carry-on when I go through security and put it on the belt so I don't get accused of breaking a law.

Being the germophobe I am, I pack little sockettes in my purse so I can put them on when I have to take off my shoes and stand on some gross, filthy carpet where thousands do the same every day. Yes, yes, I know: take off my jacket, take the battery out of my laptop before placing it on the security belt… I know all that. Is it any wonder those lines take so damn long, with all that's involved? Here's my take on scanners: two words, privacy invasion. Is anything still sacred?

As a girl who has been inhibited most of her life when it comes to undressing, I now have to step inside an x-ray machine for all of security to peruse my naked body at their leisure. Oh, and by the way, thanks for the hefty dose of radiation. It really pleases me that I'm sacrificing my health to cross the security line every time I want to travel.

And of course I remember to toss my half-empty water bottle before entering security. I'm only too happy to pay $3.79 for another one afterward. After I re-dress myself and repack everything I've sent through the scanner, my irradiated self and I can finally set off for my gate.

Returning home from a vacation is always a nerve-racking event for me. Instead of flying home and basking in the memories of the wonderful time I've just had on vacation, I repeatedly go through my receipts from the trip so I can carefully calculate how not to exceed the fixed limit we're allowed to bring back without penalty. I must remember which receipts correspond to the tags I've already cut off so I can take them out of the pile. More math!

Most people don't worry about such things—but I have to. It's practically like my face is on a milk carton: HAVE YOU SEEN THIS WOMAN SHOPPING? For decades now, I've been consistently pulled over at customs. A planeload of people pick up their luggage and sail through the exit doors to freedom, and one person (and her husband) get singled out for interrogation. This happens on ninety percent of my trips. Why is it that I'm picked out of two hundred and fifty passengers to be interrogated? I lament, but I'm familiar with all the tricks by now: don't wear flashy jewelry, don't dress up, try to blend in. I can't help it, though. I have what I've identified as *shopping face.*

When I eventually do get home and share my customs adventures with my friends, they get such a kick out of it. They insist I cannot blend in. I retort with "I wear jeans, a T-shirt, and no jewelry," but they usually just comment that I shouldn't wear makeup, either, and I should bring a baseball cap to hide my flaming red hair. Maybe I should just dye it and go in my pajamas, too? Are you kidding me? I feel as though I'm being profiled for the color of my hair!

But it is what it is, and I'm always ready for the usual proceedings when I pick up my bags. Countless times, I've been sent into the search and interrogation room at Canada customs. Sometimes they rummage through my things, and sometimes they're satisfied with my answers and my receipts. I've gotten quite good at the drill over the years. It's just a pain in the ass, and what I always feel like saying to them is "Seriously, again? You guys are worried about charging me a measly thirteen percent tax if I'm over my declaration allowance. With the money I earn, don't I have the right to spend freely on vacation without supporting the economy?"

I like to buy things we don't even have access to at home—as well as things that are considerably cheaper elsewhere! I shake my head when I think about the murderers and drug smugglers running free, but the customs guys are worried about squeezing a few more dollars out of me. These are just some of the things I'd like to say, but I wouldn't even want to think about the consequences. I've learned to keep my opinionated mouth shut to all customs officers. Canada customs in particular are sometimes very cranky people, and many love to throw their authority around. Although I certainly don't classify myself as a criminal shopper, I don't see how spending *a few* dollars more than I'm sometimes permitted constitutes a major crime. But I always seem to feel as though I'm perceived as guilty until proven innocent.

I can remember the first time my husband and I went to Las Vegas while we were dating. Naturally, we were detained when we returned home. I was used to it, but he'd never been questioned by customs. They ransacked my belongings as though they were looking for gold. My husband was livid and started making rude remarks to them, asking them if they got off going through my underwear. I was mortified and scared they would handcuff him and take him away, so I kicked him so hard in the shin while we stood there, being reprimanded by the officer for his remark, that he got the message fast. He shut up.

When we finally got out of there, I told my husband straight out, "I should have warned you, this always happens to me. If you're going to remain in my life, you'd better get used to it."

A word about TSA locks: pardon me for asking, but isn't the reason we pay for those special locks so that the TSA can open them with their master keys? So why the heck do they persist in cutting off my locks completely and sometimes even breaking my zippers? Can they please use a little common courtesy? It's getting a little costly to keep having to buy new luggage after every trip. Thanks!

Heading South

As the guidelines for travel slowly became stricter, I at first tended to disregard them, thinking I could still get away with my old travel tricks. The first time I realized the gig was up was on a trip to Miami en route to a Caribbean cruise.

My husband and I were checking in at the airport when a cranky Air Canada agent sternly asked us to put our luggage on the scale. He promptly informed us that one of our bags was seven pounds overweight. Apparently, at the time, less than five pounds overweight constituted an extra fee of approximately fifty dollars. But over five pounds brought the surcharge fee up to almost one hundred! I was furious but tried my best to conceal it, as I hoped to get on the agent's better side, to no avail. He advised us that he had to flag the overweight bag by putting a sticker on it to notify the baggage handlers that the bag was over fifty pounds.

It is apparently a union regulation that baggage handlers cannot lift anything over fifty pounds without being informed. The agent also *kindly* suggested that I could pull some items out of the bag and put them into the lighter bag or perhaps in my carry-on. At least he offered some consolation! But let me tell you how embarrassing it was holding up the check-in line while I opened my suitcase for the world to see as I rummaged for items that would total seven pounds.

I pulled out my toiletry bag, which had to have weighed at least five pounds, and a couple pairs of shoes, and I relocated them and was good to go. Then I took my bags, my humiliation, and myself and proceeded down to customs.

It was only after that incident that I began to pay attention to the seriousness of the new guidelines and invested in a portable luggage scale. After adapting to the new system, I will admit there are still incidents where I have to deal with overweight luggage, and I have to think quick about how I'm going to get all my wares home sans surcharge—for example, whenever I go on a cruise that departs from Florida. My largest shopping purchases are made in Florida, before I even get on the cruise. But now, being well versed in the new regulations, I've become a prepared shopper.

My husband and I began flying with WestJet quite a few years ago because they are friendly, competitively priced, and, until last year, allowed us each two free fifty-pound bags plus two carry-on items. (This has since changed to one free bag, depending on the fare.)

Traveling with me is never a light experience. A typical trip to Florida for a few days and a two-week cruise requires a lot of strategic suitcase planning, but I have it almost down to an art. My husband and I each take a large thirty-inch suitcase for our clothes, a third bag for all of our formal evening wear on the ship, and a fourth bag that contains all of my toiletries, drugstore aids, a blow dryer (because I like my own), hot rollers, a curling iron, books, and whatever else I can fit in. We each also take a carry-on bag, and my big purse counts for my second carry-on. Granted, this is only until the return portion of our trip, when my husband adopts a second carry-on containing all my extra purchases. Take that, airlines!

I'm now on top of my game while staying perfectly within all the guidelines and restrictions. Well… except maybe for one other large shopping excursion in Las Vegas with my friend Mary.

Me, My Shoes, and I

My big mistake on this trip to Vegas was thinking that because I was only going for five days, I was being practical by only taking one suitcase and a carry-on. I could have taken two suitcases, but I had enough space in my one bag going down, and I was grateful not to have to tow two of them. Being a seasoned shopper, I knew there would be a lot of walking in Vegas, and because I didn't want to have to cart around bags all day at the mall, I packed a large vinyl tote with wheels attached to take with me on shopping days.

As it turns out, that bag saved me both from schlepping numerous bags around the mall and probably from one hundred dollars in overweight luggage fees on my return home.

It could have all been avoided if I hadn't hit a five-hundred-dollar win at the *Breakfast at Tiffany's* slot machine outside the Starbucks where Mary and I planted ourselves to drink our morning coffee. I drank my coffee, cashed my ticket, and headed straight to the mall. I went there to purchase the Michael Kors purse

I had previously been drooling over after leaving it behind, along with four pairs of shoes I'd also been sad to leave behind after already having purchased four pairs.

Yes, yes, okay...I'm a shoe freak, I admit it. But when the time came to pack up and go home, I got a rude awakening. Not only was my suitcase severely overweight, it wouldn't even close. It was at that time that WestJet began charging for a second bag, and I didn't want to have to buy another suitcase and pay to check it, so I had to come up with a plan to get all my purchases home with me.

I decided to put the heaviest items, the shoes, into the vinyl wheely bag and pass it off as a second carry-on (also placing my purse in it to avoid having three carry-on items). I was quite concerned about the two-foot height of that bag, because in its full size it was also too big for carry-on regulations. But I had a plan! I loaded several pairs of shoes into the bag, and as Mary and I busted a gut in laughter, I thanked God for those wheels. The shoes only filled half the bag, and my plan was to wheel my two carry-ons through the airport. When it came time to board the plane, though, I was determined not to display the vinyl bag's largeness for everyone to see.

I folded it down as far as I could and stood in the boarding line with it in my hand, trying my best to look nonchalant, as though it was merely a second little carry-on. All the while, my back was killing me! It was so heavy that it was agonizing just for me to carry it to board the plane. If I were to get caught and asked to weigh it, the plan would backfire. But nobody knew the difference, and I got on the plane without question.

Yes, I am one crazy girl, but I will resort to doing whatever's necessary to get all my belongings home without added expense.

Tipping the Scales,
Too Many Sales

When my best friend Zan and I get together, we often reminisce about our past adventures. We've been besties for well over three decades now, and together we've had a lot of crazy fun times. It's pretty much standard for Zan to comment with her infamous saying, "What happened to twenty-five?" every time we recall a funny experience we've shared while trying to account for the years gone by. I'm fortunate to have had such a fun-filled, adventurous life with good friends.

I've done so many crazy things in my life, but some of my most memorable moments have taken place with Zan and my other bestie, Bri. With them I've laughed, cried, traveled, and practically lived in each of their homes at times.

I love to laugh, and apparently my sense of humor affords me the ability to make others laugh, too. I love to share stories, and I'm known to be very animated when telling them. I've also invented quite a vocabulary of made-up words and expressions that have stuck around for years. Many of these words have no sense or value to the average listener, but between my best friends and me, they remain a constant part of our lingo, especially when it comes to humor.

Some may interpret them as code words, because surely they aren't words anyone would find in an English dictionary—or in any dictionary, for that matter. Suffice it to say, many spectators have raised an eyebrow to some of our outbursts in public situations. We hopefully left them not only scratching their heads but enjoying a few giggles, too. I have to laugh as I'm writing this and remembering the time I went to visit Zan after she moved to London, England. I went there with my extremely large plaid suitcase, which was already practically full. After too much shopping (an eternal weakness), we both had to sit on the bag while Zan struggled to zip it closed for my journey home.

In those times, back in the mid '90s, the airlines weren't quite as strict as they've become in today's world. Nonetheless, there were still weight restrictions, and guidelines weren't something I adhered to very well. We didn't have a scale at the time, but I knew it instinctively. The fact that the two of us together could barely lift that bag into the car was a big indicator that my bag well exceeded the permitted weight. But I was thrilled with my purchases and thought nothing of it other than expecting, at most, to be hit up for an overweight fee.

Zan and I laughed about my obsessive shopping habit all the way to the airport. Truth be told, I was a bit concerned about how we were going to lift that bag onto the scale at check-in without blatantly struggling. Back in those days, though, they didn't always weigh the luggage. If necessary, I planned for us to look casual as we heaved the bag onto the platform so as not to cause any attention or curiosity from the ticket agent.

As we neared my turn to check in, I became a little nervous about pulling off nonchalance with my suitcase. Zan and I plotted. We decided that if we flirted with the agent, we might be able to divert his attention from my ginormous suitcase. Well, it was finally my turn, and we were doing a reasonable job of holding the agent's attention with our almost nonsensical banter until he asked me to place my bag on the scale before he could send it to the luggage hold. He couldn't help but notice how the two of us struggled to lift the bag only a mere eight inches off the ground up to the platform in front of us. At that moment, I knew I was going to be in for a hefty overweight tax.

He cast his eyes on my bag, took a few steps over to assist us as he noticed our struggle, and attempted to lift my bag onto the scale by himself. In an instant, he decided not to bother. He shook his head with a shifty smile, opened his desk drawer, and pulled out a huge red sticker. The sticker was marked in big, bold letters: HEAVY LIFTING. He proceeded to tape the sticker on the front of my bag, got another person to help him get my bag directly on the luggage belt, smiled at me, handed me my boarding pass, and wished me a safe journey home.

The size of that bag alone, even without the weight

taken into consideration, would make it an illegal suitcase today, given the strict dimensional guidelines of allowable checked luggage. Today's restrictions on weight, size, and how many bags we're allowed, and all the accompanying fees, have really put a damper on and created a huge challenge out of my packing regime. All the new rules and airline restrictions have certainly hindered my passion for packing everything I feel I need to take with me on a trip, and they have me constantly trying to come up with alternative, more efficient packing methods.

London Times

Zan moved to London, England, about two decades ago. Holy cow, again I am gob smacked at how fast the time has passed. Zan and I are each other's yin and yang. We bring out the humor in each other, and it seems that everywhere we go, we have an uncanny ability to leave a lasting impression in our tracks. Sure, some would say it's my flaming red hair and Zan's blond bombshell appearance that cause heads to turn, but when we're together, people can't help but notice loud laughter and strange dialogue coming from our direction.

When Zan gets excited about something, her decibel level goes up, and I in turn have to raise my own voice to be heard over hers. Many times, if I find Zan's volume getting too elevated, I will reach for her ear in an effort to pretend I'm turning down a volume knob. She'll quickly realize and lower her tone, which of course sets us both off on a new fit of laughter.

Zan and I are both admitted shopaholics. I can't even count the numerous times our shopping habits have drained us of our last ounces of energy while leaving our unintentionally humorous imprint behind in the stores we've visited. Our laughter and occasional lack of volume control in our shopping adventures have undoubtedly left many onlookers no choice but to stare at us and often enjoy a chuckle at our antics.

When Zan first moved to the United Kingdom, she lived in a lovely condo in the Docklands. It was a beautiful area with a stunning view of the Thames. Needless to say, we did a lot of shopping together, and thanks to Zan's great tour guide abilities, she took me to see many historic parts of London.

One day, while we were touring downtown London, we passed through Piccadilly Circus and Trafalgar Square and many other landmarks. We were planning to make our way over to Buckingham Palace—or Buckhouse, as Zan prefers to call it—but we somehow ended up at another royal building. At that point, we had managed to lose our bearings, or maybe I should say that Zan had, considering I was completely lost all the time.

Whatever it was, Zan admitted that she was having a blond moment. She seemed to have lost her direction, and instead of asking any passersby for directions, she opted to consult a Beefeater, a royal guard who happened to be standing at attention in front of the gate. He was fully garbed in his Beefeater hat, kilt, and chin guard, staring sternly straight ahead. I was certain he was tempted to crack a smile as he listened to the two of us nattering to each other about our dilemma while we tried to figure out where we were. It's protocol for these guards to remain stoic without conveying physical emotion or conversing while on duty.

Zan unabashedly walked up to him with one hand posed on her hip while her other hand aided in articulating her question to him in her true animated style. "Um, excuse me. Where are we? We were hoping to get to Buckingham Palace," she asked matter of factly.

The guard couldn't help but smile and offer us directions. We still roar about this today. Only Zan would have the chutzpah to approach a guard on active duty.

Another day, Zan and I ventured off to a big shopping mall just outside of London. We spent the better part of the day going into several stores, and by later that afternoon, as per usual, we were carting around several shopping bags. Just as we were complaining to one another about how tired our feet were, we spotted a row of what appeared to be La-Z-Boy reclining chairs smack in the middle of the mall. It was obvious that these chairs were there for promotion. The selling feature on them was a built-in massager in the back of the recliner. The chairs were there for anyone to try out—and, I'm sure, to entice sales. We thought we'd take the opportunity to rest our weary selves for a few moments.

While other shoppers passed us by, destined for their favorite stores, Zan and I put our bags down and leaned back into the chairs with the massagers turned on. For a few moments, we reveled in the great relief our tired bones were experiencing, so much that we barely remembered we were in a public place. Simultaneously, we both began to moan in ecstasy. In unison, we both sat up when we realized how we must have sounded to the people walking by. Of course, there were many shoppers stopping in their tracks to watch us bask in our hilarity. I often compare that moment to the famed restaurant scene in *When Harry Met Sally* when Sally fakes an orgasm to prove to Harry that women can be good fakers.

Another day, our shopping travels led us to Covent Garden. This was a lovely area in London with an array of open markets. While I was having a look at the many wares, I encountered a little incident. I will preface this incident by reiterating the point that I'm a germophobe. I was admiring some knickknacks, and something of interest caught my eye. I reached out to pick up the object of interest, and in that exact moment, a big, dirty seagull flew by and crapped on my hand. I was mortified, and I became hysterical, shouting to get Zan's attention at a nearby table. I screamed, "Oh my God, Zan, a bird just shit on my hand. CUT IT OFF! CUT OFF MY HAND!"

My horrified cries had captured much more than the attention of my friend and had provided ample entertainment to the many surrounding shoppers. Zan came running to my aid, fully armed with Kleenex and wet wipes, but not before nearly falling to the ground in a grand fit of laughter.

Paired in Paris

Often, when I went to visit Zan, we took little trips to other countries. One of our favorites was our jaunt to Paris. By that time, Zan was living in Kent, near Ashford.

Zan's husband, Taylor, was doing business in Paris at the time, and he invited us to join him on a three-day trip there. His only requirement was that we stay in a different hotel—away from him. We were elated. Zan may have become a British subject, but she sure never lost the Canadian in her spirit, and although Taylor was himself a man with a good sense of humor, he wasn't loud like us and wasn't into being part of our spectacle, which he knew quite well by that point.

Left on our own, with full intentions of shopping, Zan and I spent three glorious days walking the streets of Paris, taking in the Parisian lifestyle and fashion. Our first day, we walked for nearly seven hours. Rain began to fall, and still we kept walking. Later in the day, I discovered a hole in the bottom of my shoe after sensing that my left sock felt damp. It wasn't nearly late enough to end our shopping expedition, so we immediately went in search of a shoe store. It wasn't hard to find one, as there were plenty of them nearby as we strolled the Champs-Élysées.

While I was trying on shoes in a store we had wandered into, Zan was only too happy to be doing the same. It was difficult for her to find shoes she liked, because she has big feet. While I admired and tried on various shoes, I could hear Zan's voice loud and clear from the other end of the vast store. With a comical tone in her voice, she was asking the salesperson, "Um, excuse me, but do these shoes come with oars?"

Tears of laughter immediately spawned from my eyes as I struggled to breathe through my fit of laughter, still listening as Zan continued to explain to the clerk that the shoes she was trying on tended to look as though she was wearing a pair of canoes.

We finally purchased a pair of shoes each and continued walking. We barely took the time to stop and eat, not much more than a coffee and a croissant before we started our day, but Zan had reservations for dinner in a lovely restaurant that she and her husband frequented when in Paris. It was getting late after our long day, and we needed to get back to the hotel to change for dinner.

When we returned to our beautiful Marie Antoinette-esque suite overlooking the Louvre, we both plopped our numerous bags down. Simultaneously, we flopped down on the bed, faced one another, and blurted out, "Room service." We were exhausted and ravenously hungry. Neither of us had the strength to get dressed and walk to the restaurant, and we decided we should stay in and get a good night's rest so we could wake up in the morning and do it all over again.

At the end of that fabulous trip, after three days in Paris, we got back on the train in Calais that took us back to Ashford, England, via the Channel Tunnel, frequently referred to as the Chunnel. With the amount of bags we had accumulated from our shopping frenzy, one might have presumed we'd been away for weeks. We laughed incessantly on the train about our experience as Taylor held a newspaper up close in front of his face, reading, all the while pretending not to know us.

By then, Zan and I were so giddy that everything we said and did made us laugh. We both knew that Taylor was getting a bit annoyed with our loud outbursts of hysterics, but everyone knows how hard it is to stop laughing when you know you should be quiet. We arrived back in Ashford, and we were getting ready to get off the train. Zan and I were trying our best to stop laughing to avoid attracting attention, as we felt the tension in the air as Taylor reached the end of his patience. We tried hard to keep a straight face and not look at one another, as we knew we only had to catch each other's eyes once and we were going to explode into laughter.

A kindly porter offered his hand to help us disembark the train and aid us with our bags. He tipped his hat at us, smiled, and said, "I hope you had a lovely time in Paris, ladies. I see you've done a little shopping."

That was it! That was our breaking point. We could no longer stay silent. Zan and I looked at each other and, in unison, replied, "Yes, just a little."

In that moment, we set our bags down and let out the howls of laughter we had so desperately tried to conceal before exiting the train. We laughed so hard our mascara was streaming down our faces, leaving tiny droplets of black tears in our trail. Taylor grabbed what he could hold of our bags and proceeded to walk in haste, well ahead, in an effort to avoid letting anyone think he was with us. We laughed all the way through to security.

Once at security, they stopped Taylor for a quick check. A security agent asked him to open one of the bags he was carrying. Guess whose bag it was?

A Different Ride

Ever since Zan and I became best friends around age twenty, we've been like glue. We did everything together and shared a great circle of friends. We all hung out together, went on little outings together, and attended numerous parties. Zan has always been protective of me. Although I'm five months older than she is, I've always felt she's like a big sister to me.

In the earlier days of our friendship, she and our friends loved to tease me about my shortcomings. I knew I was loved and it was all in fun, and I joined in the laughter because I was usually pretty much asking for it. I seemed to be the one who provided a lot of entertainment just by my nature and crazy quirks.

We had so many friends between us, and we were both welcomed into all of their lives. I once worked with a friend named Tom. He was a photographer, and his family owned a mostly vacant cottage up in Muskoka, cottage country. Tom invited Zan, me, and a bunch of our friends up to his cottage a few times to spend the weekend. Now those were good times! It was mostly wintertime when we'd go up there. There were always plenty of outdoor activities to engage in for those who wished to indulge. At night, we'd have some drinks and play board games. I enjoyed the nighttime parties much more than the physical outdoor activities.

One particular Sunday morning, I was awakened by Zan and her boyfriend tackling me, pinning me down, and dressing me up warm over my pajamas in some unknown person's ski suit. They carried me onto the garbage lid outside, which Tom had tied to the back of his car. This plan, hatched by my friends, had been set up in retaliation for my never wanting to participate in any outdoor activities. I didn't like the cold, and I was not a skier. I was much happier staying back by the fireplace while they went out to exhaust themselves.

Nonetheless, their plan was to take me for a slippery manmade toboggan ride down the icy street. After my refusal to participate in many activities, they had decided it was payback time. It actually turned out to be a lot of fun, with laughs galore.

Whenever Zan and I get together, we can't help but reminisce over the things we've endured and enjoyed. That woman has been very instrumental in getting me to expand my horizons, take chances, and learn to savor the little moments in life.

We talk about our good times often, as though they've occurred only recently. Somehow, we don't feel the years that have passed in between. We reminisce as though we're still young girls. Every time we talk about *those days,* we shake our heads in disbelief when we remember that we're both now nearing our mid fifties. And after reminiscing about a story, one of us will always say, "What happened to twenty-five?"

Hot Weather,
Beautiful Leather

My cousin Eileen and I decided to take a trip to Venezuela. We often hung out together, and both of us, being single at the time, thought it would be a great trip to get away for some sun, fun, and shopping.

In my crazy younger days, there were a few pre-requisites I had before choosing a destination for vacation: it had to be a hot and sunny place, and it had to include good shopping and prices. Our two destinations, Margarita Island and Caracas, Venezuela, fit the bill.

Our fun began on the flight down, as we happened to befriend a pilot and copilot who were flying as passengers. We had many laughs, and those guys seemed to take quite a shining to my cousin and me as the five-and-a-half-hour flight passed. Before we deplaned, Eileen and I agreed to have dinner with them the following night.

The next day, we were on the beach, soaking up

some of the hottest rays I can ever remember taking in—no doubt, being so close to the equator. As we sipped on our tropical drinks and basked in the sun, we heard a lot of laughter coming from nearby. We turned our heads to follow the sound, and we later discovered that a flight crew from Alitalia airlines was spending a few days' layover at our same hotel. It wasn't long before they invited us to come sit with them and join them for a few drinks.

After a day at the pool with our newfound friends, a few of the guys invited us to meet them later in the evening at the hotel bar. We told them we had plans that evening and would be happy to meet them the next night. Later that evening, our pilot and copilot friends showed up to take us for dinner. We got on well with them but had no romantic interest. We saw them as just some nice dinner company.

After dinner, we had a few more drinks, and while Eileen and the pilot were engaged in conversation, I was trying to keep the other guy at bay, as he became very touchy-feely and repeatedly tried to kiss me. I eventually came up with an exit plan, and he got the hint.

The next day, out at the pool, we had a ton of fun back with our Alitalia friends. They were an entertaining bunch of fellows, and they were very respectful toward us. Okay, so maybe one of them came on to me and another to my cousin, but they weren't offensive or pushy, and there was certainly no harm in flirting. That night, the guys had a party in their room and invited us. They even allowed me to try on their airline uniform, complete with pilot's cap. I still have those hilarious pictures.

After a fun-filled five days on Margarita Island, we went off to Caracas for another five days. We were warned not to go about the city on our own without a so-called bodyguard, as the crime rate had made it particularly dangerous for tourists—and we most definitely looked like tourists. We were told to be especially on guard at shopping malls. "What?" I retorted. I couldn't possibly fathom the thought that I needed an escort just to do some shopping. I had heard that Venezuela had beautiful leather designer shoes for ridiculously cheap prices. Purchasing a few pairs of those babies was definitely on my agenda!

It turned out that the cab driver who drove us to the mall offered us his escort services. He carried our many bags and drove us back to the hotel after, spending the day with us for a cheap rate of twenty dollars. I was in shoe heaven and found myself four pairs of Charles Jourdan shoes, along with a few other pairs from various designers. Those shoes were stunning, sexy, and stylish, and the retail prices were just as beautiful.

At that time, over three decades ago, it was exceedingly cheap to vacation in Venezuela. It was also known for having some of the best beef in the world, and no doubt that was why the leather was also impeccable. I recall going out one night for a beautiful steak dinner and couldn't get over how my bill was something crazy, like five dollars! Those certainly were the days.

Suffice it to say, Eileen and I had a fantastic time on

that trip. I returned home darker than I'd ever been and many pairs of shoes richer.

My other best friend, Bri, lived across the street from me at the time, and I asked her if she'd pick me up from the airport when I returned—but she took on a bit more than she had bargained for when she arrived at the airport.

Eileen and I picked up our luggage and proceeded to walk out through customs when a hand was posed in front of my face, alerting me that I wasn't walking out with her. As Eileen leaned over to hug me goodbye, she whispered, "Good luck." She left me, and I was petrified I might be going to shoe jail.

Once I was at the customs detention desk, they requested that I open all my luggage. I was grilled about the many things I had brought back, including some of my own things that I had actually taken with me on that trip. As they sifted through my belongings, they kept finding yet more pairs of shoes. I can't exactly recall how many pairs of shoes I bought, but it was somewhere in the neighborhood of eight. I tried to joke around, hoping my friendly smile and demeanor might soften the officer's authoritative attitude—not unlike what many women try to do to get out of a speeding ticket.

An hour had already passed, and I was still in that so-called holding tank. I was getting concerned because I had yet to learn that I should have been keeping receipts to verify the value of what I'd bought. I was fearful that customs would be placing their own perceived value on my goods without my having actual proof. Those shoes would have well exceeded the legal declaration limits if they were priced at what they would have cost in an expensive designer boutique in Toronto.

More time passed, and I was eyeing my beautiful new shoes, which were now lined up on the customs desk, wondering if I'd even be able to take my prized possessions home, when it dawned on me. As I held one of the shoes in my hand as if searching for some miraculous sign, I turned the shoe over to admire its beautiful leather sole, and there it was. Engraved into the bottom of the sole was the actual price of the shoes in native bolivars, the currency used in Venezuela.

I sighed in relief. I pointed out my revelation to the officer, who went to look up the conversion rates from bolivars to dollars and came back with a calculator. I could tell by the shocked look on his face that he couldn't believe how cheap my beautiful shoes really were.

However, in those days, our customs allowance was pretty meager. Even with the cheap prices I had paid, I was still over the allowable limit. After all the calculations were done, the officer gave me his little speech. He informed me that although I was over the limit, I had brought this clever method of verifying the price of shoes from Venezuela to his attention. This, of course, gave him ammunition to nab the next poor shoe victim who would have the pleasure of being detained. He finally allowed me to repack my bags and go home.

When I finally got out of that situation and walked

out the exit doors, I was elated to see my pal Bri, still out there all by her lonesome, waiting for me to get out of customs. She knew instinctively that her shoe-loving friend had, once again, been detained for interrogation.

Slipping in Greece

It took me many trips before I learned my lessons on how to pack more efficiently. Until I garnered my experience, I often struggled to transport my luggage.

Imagine a young girl of twenty-five taking a three-month leave of absence to travel the Greek islands alone. Now visualize her carting three suitcases around, on and off ferryboats, and walking through narrow cobblestone lanes just to find a taxi. Yup, that was me. And, of course, I had that overly large plaid suitcase with me, which I later took to London. Was I even normal?

I'd convinced myself that because I was going for three months and would be renting a villa where I could leave my bags and travel to other islands, I was not a backpacker. This allowed me to take everything I felt I'd need. Did I consult with anyone? No. Did I even begin to think about how inconvenient this would make traveling from place to place? No! I was very independent (and stubborn), and nobody's advice would have changed my thinking.

My bags barely fit in the small European taxis in Athens. Just getting to the hotel was a struggle, as was fitting them in and on the car. But those were the least of my baggage woes. I'd had grand illusions of cruise ships when I booked my passage to Mykonos. I found out that they weren't so grand. Many narrow steps led up to the ferry. No, there were no handsome officers waiting to escort me and my bags up those steps. I, in fact, had to bribe some dockworker with cash to take my bags up for me on the overnight sail to the island. Getting back off the ship was just as disastrous.

By the time I hailed a cab at port to my rented accommodations in Mykonos, I was still seasick and melting in the sweltering forty-two-degree Celsius heat wave. Alas, I was on my way to the villa, and when I arrived, my eyes scanned what seemed like the small mountaintop where I'd be staying. There was no walkway, rather a dusty path interspersed with weeds and the odd cement stepping-stone. Once again, it cost me extra money to pay the poor and very old taxi driver to drag my bags up the hill.

Once settled, I knew that any other excursions I'd be taking would definitely involve leaving most of my things behind and packing lightly in one of the smaller suitcases to boat over to another island. As it turned out, I broke my foot a week later, after slipping off a very high step while exiting a bus. That inconvenience had me spending the remainder of that vacation planted on a one-island destination. That incident left me having to figure out a packing strategy only one more time, and worrying about how I would get my burden of bags down the steep hill when it was time to go home.

Minnesota: I'll Take a Pass on the Mayo

My father wasn't well by the time he hit his mid forties. He had already suffered a stroke and a heart attack and had terribly high cholesterol levels. His poor eating habits only added to his declining health.

I was very protective of my dad, and I wanted to have him checked out thoroughly. I finally convinced him to go to the Mayo Clinic in Rochester, Minnesota, for a thorough checkup, and he agreed to go if I would go with him. So there we were, off to freezing cold Minnesota in the depths of January winter.

We had only planned to be there for a few days, so I didn't feel the need to take the jumbo plaid suitcase with me. I opted for one size down. Nonetheless, it was quite an adventure getting there, as we had to connect from Toronto into Chicago's O'Hare airport. Anyone who has been to O'Hare knows very well how big and busy that place is, with its many terminals.

By the time our plane landed, after delays, we found that we had landed in terminal two and had

forty-five minutes left to catch our connecting flight…
in terminal three! I was stunned when I figured out
that this timeframe was almost impossible to adhere
to, and I had to think fast. My father was quite able
to walk, but that was about it. This mission required
some Olympic running on both our parts, and I knew
that wasn't about to happen.

I immediately ran and got a wheelchair. I ordered
my father to get in, and then I began running like a
fart in the wind, pushing my dad to the finish line. I
can still remember the teal blue skirt and jacket I had
on and, of course, my high heels. Sweating and out of
breath, we made it to the plane without a minute to
spare.

After we got off the plane, we waited at the luggage
carousel for our bags. After some time, my dad's suitcase came off, but mine had yet to make an appearance. Finally, after what seemed like an hour, there it
was—opened up completely, displaying my wardrobe
and personal items for the world to see.

Not only was the suitcase completely unzipped and
left open, there was a huge black tire tread embedded
across my clothes from one end to the other. I was
livid. Who does that? Who opens a suitcase before it
gets on the luggage belts and runs over it with some
unknown vehicle?

Dad and I lifted off the carousel what now looked
like an open-faced sandwich of clothes and found
the zipper completely broken, which left the suitcase
unable to close. We then had to go looking for security
to find some way to tie my suitcase so we could get it to

the hotel without having to hold it upright. The whole situation was bizarre, and with all that the suitcase had endured, I was more than happily surprised that every single item I'd packed was still there!

By no means was that a leisure trip. I had no prior intentions of shopping in that frosty state—one of the coldest places I can remember being in. But I did have to go out searching for a store to buy a new suitcase just so I could get my things back home.

Las Vegas, Then and Now

L   as Vegas was once a magical place with a hint
of mystique. At least that's the way I remember
it. The first time I went there and the wheels of
the airplane touched down at McCarran airport, the
vast desert and the red rock mountains mesmerized
me. I was mystified by the small desert town that I had
come to identify as a land of make believe, an adult
wonderland, a secret forbidden fruit. My fascination
with old mob movies coupled with the glamorous life-
styles of movie stars had me brimming with excitement for what awaited me in that hidden little world
in the desert.

I was twenty when I first visited Las Vegas. The
legal gambling and drinking age there is twenty-one,
but that was never an issue for me, as I dressed and
looked as though I was well into my twenties. It was
Christmastime in 1979. The days of old Las Vegas were
fading, and the town was barely a decade away from
expanding into the metropolis it has now become.
Vegas was on the precipice, hanging on to its iconic

stars, soon to be converted into a place where bigger was better, where each hotel would be torn down and rebuilt bigger than the last.

My mother was dating a fellow who ran junkets to Las Vegas once a month. The die-hard gamblers who were willing to commit to a certain amount of dollars could practically fly free and have their rooms comped, and they often received much more, such as food and free tickets to shows. Drinks were always free in the casinos. If you proved yourself a worthy gambler, you'd be treated like a queen or king.

On this particular trip, there happened to be an extra empty seat available on the plane, as my mother's boyfriend wasn't taking that trip. I was quite surprised and elated when she invited me to keep her company, so I didn't hesitate to go. My curiosity was piqued.

I had heard the desert temps were considerably cooler at that time of year, so I packed some fall clothes for the trip, but it turned out to be an unseasonably warm winter. The usual mid-fifties temperatures were tipping the mercury in the mid eighties. It was dry and hot, and I reveled in the heat. A beautiful boutique in the lobby of the Flamingo Hotel caught my attention, and it didn't take me long to find some beautiful things and a bathing suit, which I came to need unexpectedly to go to the pool.

It was a five-minute drive (in those days) from the airport to what's known as the hotel strip. I can still recall how amazed I was while the limo drove us down what was then not much more than a big dirt road with iconic hotels spread out along the way, interspersed with tumbleweeds and cacti and empty parcels of land. The strip was nothing more than the hotels that stood there and the magical world inside each of them.

I nicknamed Las Vegas Tip City. Everybody worked for tips, which were a mandatory unspoken gesture. Anyone that requested anything tipped. You tipped the taxi drivers, the doormen, the jockey who opened your taxi door, the concierge, and just about anyone who provided even the most minimal service. Heck, even the bathrooms had attendants who waited for you to come out of the stall and wash your hands so they could personally hand you a paper towel and cop a dollar. No, they don't tell you that you have to tip, but you are certainly frowned upon as a cheap ass if you don't.

Oh yes, those were the good old days in Vegas. All the glamor and glitz and the beautiful people, it was euphoric. In those days, men and women dressed in their finest attire at night, usually black tie. I adored it. The men looked dashing in their tuxedos, and the women often donned gowns, their bodies decorated with jewels as though they were at some grand ball. I was in fashion heaven.

My mother gave me a black chip to use for gambling. Black chips are valued at one hundred dollars. I got myself comfortable at a one-dollar minimum bet blackjack table. I had won and lost my dollar bets back and forth for three days on that same one hundred dollars. The air was thick with excitement and smoke. Sleep wasn't a requirement due to the excitement and the oxygen being pumped in the casino vents to keep you awake, complete with free drinks. The drinks were a gesture to keep everyone happy and playing—and, I surmised, tipsy enough to make bad gambling decisions. But that was all part of the Vegas charm.

Casinos have no clocks or windows. In that environment, time doesn't matter. It was a magical escape from real life. It wasn't uncommon to spot a movie star walking through the casino during the day or in between shows. I went to see Liberace perform, and his elaborate costumes and candelabra made me feel as though I was living in a Hollywood storybook. Another night, I swayed to Paul Anka belting out "Puppy Love" and "Diana."

It was an exciting time, and I was hooked. Years passed, but my love for Vegas never faltered. The same feeling I experienced on my first trip to Vegas still overcame me when my feet hit Nevada soil during every consequent trip I made to that desert town. I went back a few more times with my mother while I was in my twenties, then several times with my own friends in my thirties. It was in the late eighties, early nineties when I really began to see the Vegas I had known evolve into a metropolis.

Each time I went back to Vegas, I saw how much the city was growing. The population was increasing, with many new people migrating there. The once old dirt road, Las Vegas Boulevard, was paved with new lanes to accommodate the bumper-to-bumper traffic. Slowly but surely, through the nineties, iconic hotels imploded. The mystique of the past began going up in dynamite. The infamous hotels were replaced by bigger and supposedly better newer ones. But that is a matter of personal opinion.

In the olden days, the casino dealers wore costumes to reflect the theme of their hotels. I used to love going to the Aladdin Hotel with my sister to play bingo. The Aladdin was one of the very few hotels at the time to offer bingo, and it was a fun place to go and play for not a lot of money, with the potential to win some big prizes. After bingo, we'd go into the casino to play some cards. The décor was Mesopotamian throughout, complete with pillars and wall art, all following the genie theme. Even the dealers wore genie costumes. Their balloon-sleeved shirts and harem pants added to the fairy tale atmosphere.

In 2006, after not having gone to Vegas for a few years, I went back with my girlfriend Bri. She knew how much I loved Vegas, because I had told her so many stories about it. I had told her that the hotels all had a theme, and I couldn't wait to take her to the Aladdin to show her how colorful it was. When we got there, my enthusiasm vanished as soon as I saw the marquee half torn down and under construction. But the hotel was still open, halfway through being converted to what is now Planet Hollywood. We went inside, and my excitement waned further when I saw the dealers wearing standard black pants and crisp white shirts. I felt sad for the loss of the fantasy feel the hotel had once given off.

I immediately went into investigative mode and began questioning some cocktail servers, asking them what was going on. I remember one response in particular. A waitress told me that some of the hotel investors wouldn't tolerate an Arabian theme after 9/11. Personally, I had never perceived that hotel as Arabian or anything else political but rather as an entertaining storybook environment. I shook my head in disbelief while thinking about how sorry I felt for what the world was becoming.

As the years continued to pass, my husband and I went back to Vegas several times. We both love the weather and the abundance of action there, whether in the casinos or just walking down the busy strip. I became passionate about playing tournament poker, and had taken several jaunts myself and with friends to play, and to watch the World Series of Poker, which takes place there every summer.

Gone now are the once cheap "all you can eat" buffets and steak and egg breakfasts for $1.99. Vegas used to be relatively cheap, but it's become a very expensive tourist destination. In its heyday, you would never see children in Vegas. It was like an adult wonderland. Now the streets are busy with baby carriages, kids, and the younger generation. Hotel rooftops host beach parties, and nightclubs that cater to young adults are the big attraction now. The once famed nightclubs with the likes of Frank Sinatra, Sammy Davis Junior, et al. have grown into huge theaters hosting today's pop stars, along with deejays and dance clubs.

Sure, the boomers of yesterday, like myself, still love it, but we are no longer the majority there. The younger generation populates Vegas now. I'm not saying that I wasn't young when I first began going to Vegas, but I was the minority then. Vegas wasn't a child-friendly or teenage-oriented environment. And certainly, at the young age of twenty, I shouldn't have been allowed to play in the casinos either.

Comps are no longer given out as freely as they were in the past, if at all. Construction never seems to cease in efforts to keep expanding the strip and the city. And if you aren't playing in a casino where drinks are free, a bottle of water can run you close to four dollars. Vegas is an entertainment capital as much as, or even more than, a gambling place.

After returning from our most recent trip to Las Vegas, my husband and I are now thinking it will probably be our last one—or at least a long time until we go back. It's time to move on. My love for the desert still lives, but it's definitely time to try out a new town for my short desert jaunts. As I looked around the surroundings of my once favorite place, it became quite evident that the demographics and the whole mystique had definitely changed.

As our trip neared its end, my husband and I were sitting outside a lovely café near the Paris Hotel, having a light dinner. I watched in wonder at the crazy busy sidewalks, crowded with the younger generation fighting their way through the street. Most of them had their eyes glued on their cell phones, walking and stopping aimlessly as they proceeded to their unparticular destinations. The nicely dressed people of old Vegas had changed. Shorts and flip-flops had become the standard dress code.

So much else had changed, too. The once spacious feel of a deserted town had now given way to the claustrophobia I experienced just having to walk a block. Las Vegas Boulevard, the strip, was continuously lined with cars and taxis moving at a snail's pace. What used to be the land of excitement for me had become mostly a verbally uncommunicative place. People lined the streets, hotels, casinos, and malls, texting away. There was usually no regard for what was in front of them. Restaurants were patronized by hungry texters, busy on their phones in between bites.

I was in a poker tournament one day, a place where, once upon a time, no cell phones were allowed at the tables. The dealer sat patiently, waiting for one of the players to throw in his cards after he announced his fold. The player said he folded but went directly back to his texting, forgetting to throw in his cards. I was getting quite irate at that point, as the dealer wasn't saying anything or dealing. The tournament clock was ticking away, and every minute was precious, as the blinds increased every ten minutes. I finally told him to throw in his cards if he wasn't playing the hand.

Lineups and wait times in some restaurants were also annoying. In one instance, we stood in line for almost an hour and watched empty tables sit with dirty dishes for almost the same length of time while very young hostesses, also attached to their cell phones, chatted among one another.

I noticed another strange phenomenon in the casinos—and believe me, I walked through plenty of them. No longer did I hear the deafening sounds of *ding, ding, ding* and the slot machines paying out. Slot machines dominate most of the casino floors in comparison to the gaming tables, but the payouts on the slot machines seem to have been minimized in relation to the amount one bets. Unless someone hits a jackpot on the rare occasion, other hits are relatively small payouts. I personally never cared for slots for the aforementioned reasons. I prefer poker because I'm in charge of my own destiny with the cards. I can play or fold and decide how to minimize my losses.

Everything in Vegas is expensive. Heck, a taxi can cost you almost five or six dollars before it even pulls out onto the strip. Sure, drinks are free in the casinos, but step outside and you won't find a glass of wine cheaper than ten bucks, which makes me laugh, because many of those wines wouldn't cost me that for the whole bottle if I were to buy them in a store.

No longer do I feel the elegance and charm the city once held for me. Human interaction almost seems like a thing of the past, with the exception of a few dealers or pit bosses always willing to give one a welcome and a smile when we sit down to play and leave a donation.

The nightclubs of yesteryear have all but disappeared. There are still plenty of comedy shows and Cirque du Soleils to go see, that is, if you're willing to spend a few hundred US dollars per couple.

Prices have escalated drastically since I was last there barely two years ago. Everyone is out to grab a buck from you. Often, you can find costumed characters standing on sidewalk corners on the busy strip. From Elvis to Spiderman and as many cartoon characters as you can imagine, everyone seems to have a gimmick. The only difference between the olden days and now is that you can't take their picture randomly anymore. You have to pay.

As I sat in that café, I began to wonder where all the boomers from the old Vegas days were now going. Sure, there were some there, like my husband and me, but the younger generation dominates the tourist sector in the modern Vegas. I imagined that perhaps my generation had moved on to different parts of Nevada, for those who love the state. Maybe they've moved on to Reno or Tahoe—definitely two places I'll consider visiting if I should decide to return. Because I love the desert and the mountains, and a little less hustle and bustle, my new love has become Arizona. Do I still love Vegas? I will say yes, but I remember it for everything it once was. I can't escape the nostalgic feeling that comes over me when I go there, and I love the desert climate, but each time I go back and watch the city grow just a little bit bigger, I feel another part of its old charm fade away.

Ironically, on what appears to be my last trip to Las Vegas, for the first time, I left with my bags approximately three pounds *underweight*.

Weighing In on Arizona

This coming winter, my husband and I will be living our dream of becoming snowbirds. As he nears retirement, we've made some adjustments to our lifestyle and living to accommodate our plans. The most notable change is that we've sold our home and are now living as renters in a lovely condominium to enable us the freedom to travel without having to worry about who will look after the house in the winter.

When we first booked the beautiful place we'll be renting in Arizona, we began making plans and decisions about what would be our most economical method of getting there. My biggest concern was how I could take all my comforts of home, along with my clothing, for two months.

We began Googling maps and routes when we decided it would be most feasible to drive there—both to support my personal belongings and to avoid the expense of having to rent a car once we arrived. Driving, we wouldn't be restricted as to how many suitcases we could bring or how much they could weigh.

We worked on the numbers, adding up the approximate costs of three nights in motels plus gas, food, and incidentals to get us from Toronto to the desert. Then we doubled those figures for the return trip home. I was quite excited about the prospect of driving through the United States to get to our beloved Arizona. We made the arrangements at the beginning of this year, and although it was winter, the brutality of the season's wrath had yet to show its face.

We then went away for a few weeks to Florida and then on a Caribbean cruise, and we talked often about how next winter we'd be out of the cold for two glorious months. Throughout our conversations, my husband would subtly bring up his concerns about driving all the way across the United States in winter. I kept reminding him how exciting it would be to see some new places along the way—and, besides, the journey was part of the fun.

The odd time, my husband would ask me if it wouldn't just be quicker to get on a plane and fly to Arizona. We would be there in less than five hours instead of spending four days each to get there and back. I pondered his question quite a few times as I weighed the pros and cons. The costs really weren't that different between driving and flying. What the journey would have cost in gas, lodging, and food both ways was certainly comparable to what it would cost to rent a car there for two months. And, as for the airfare, that wouldn't cost us, because we had enough airline points accumulated for two free tickets.

My biggest concern was how on earth was I supposed to go away for that length of time with only two suitcases, with a max allowable weight of fifty pounds each? All of my visions of packing half my summer wardrobe, my favorite pillows, a box full of books, all of my writing aids, and much more were slowly disappearing. How could I possibly get away with only two suitcases?

When we returned home from our cruise in mid February, the bitter curse of winter was in full force. While watching the American news, I had heard of a few major accidents with car pileups due to the brutal force of winter on the highways, sometimes leaving miles of cars just stranded, waiting for storms to pass. In these past few years, winters have become far harsher for much of North America. I had to reevaluate.

Once again, my husband and I sat down to chat about our plans after watching one of those dangerous car pileups, which had occurred on the same route we'd be driving the following winter. He told me that could be us next year as he pointed toward the television screen. The math no longer seemed to be a factor.

My husband reiterated how stupid it was for us to be driving alone on that long journey, especially considering the fact that he's two decades older than I am. I had envisioned actually driving a lot of the way on unfamiliar highways with potentially bad weather and unforeseen detours, and I began to feel anxiety rise within me. I had totally disregarded the fact that I'm a paranoid enough driver on the highways in my own city. My initial concern about how much stuff I could pack and take with me by driving to Arizona had suddenly become so inconsequential.

The next day, I had our flights and a car booked for our desert adventure. It only made sense that we fly. But that still left me with my central packing dilemma. Sure, I'm taking four of my biggest suitcases with me, keeping in mind they can't weigh over fifty pounds each. And sure, three of those four bags will be filled with *my* things. I'll be fitting my belongings in like pieces of a puzzle, and no doubt I'll be using that scale over and over as I add and subtract many items while endeavoring to fit as much as I can in without going over the weight guidelines.

But, heaven help me, what will I do when it's time for me to return home?

Helpful Travel Tips

- Invest in a good travel scale.

- Always pack a light sweater, even in summer. Airplanes can be quite chilly.

- Measure and weigh carry-on bags.

- Place small liquids and gels in a plastic bag for handy retrieval at security.

- Wrap breakables in a towel or T-shirt.

- Wear shoes that are easy to take off and put on at security checks.

- If you're a germ freak, wear or bring socks for shoe removal at security.

- Keep hydrated on the plane. Drink plenty of water!

- Do web check-in 24 hours prior to departure to avoid longer lines.

- Check the airline's website or sign up for mobile alerts prior to departure for delay advisories.

- If feasible, pre-book seats to avoid being separated from companions or being assigned crappy seats.

- Leave room in your bags on departure to return with random purchases.

- Have fun!

End

Thank you for taking the time to read *Have Bags, Will Travel.* If you enjoyed it, please consider telling your friends or posting a short review by going to this book's page at www.amazon.com. Word of mouth is an author's best friend and is much appreciated.

About the Author

D.G. Kaye is a Canadian author who resides in Toronto. Kaye is a nonfiction writer of memoirs about her life experiences, matters of the heart, and women's issues. Her positive outlook keeps her on track about taking life's challenges with a dose of humor.

Kaye began writing when pen and paper became the tools to express her pent-up emotions during a turbulent childhood. She journaled about her life at a young age and continued writing about the people and events she encountered, both of which left imprints and lessons.

D.G. began writing books to share her stories and inspiration. She also writes poetry and articles on natural health care.

Kaye is a big advocate for kindness and empowering women. Her favorite saying is "For every kindness, there should be kindness in return. Wouldn't that just make the world right?"

When D.G. isn't writing, she loves to read (self-help books and stories of triumph), cook (concocting new recipes), shop (only if it's a great sale), play poker (when she gets the chance), and, most of all, travel.

Kaye's next book, a sequel to *Conflicted Hearts*, will be published in 2016.

Visit D.G. Kaye's website at www.dgkayewriter.com and join her mailing list to keep up with her latest blogs and news on her upcoming books and events.

Email D.G. at d.g.kaye.writer@gmail.com

Follow D.G. on Twitter:
www.twitter.com/pokercubster

Facebook: www.facebook.com/dgkaye

Google: www.google.com/+DebbyDGKayeGies

LinkedIn: www.linkedin.com/in/dgkaye7

Friend and follow her on Goodreads:
www.goodreads.com/dgkaye

Visit her author page at
www.amazon.com/author/dgkaye7

Read excerpts from D.G.'s other books

Conflicted Hearts
www.amazon.com/dp/B00HDTPPUQ

Words We Carry
www.amazon.com/dp/B00KWANPZK

MenoWhat? A Memoir
www.amazon.com/dp/B00OQJGE42